THE ARCHERY FOR BEGINNERS GUIDEBOOK

CONTENTS

Welcome...

to the beginners' guide to archery. So what's so great about archery? It's the ultimate family friendly sport. It doesn't matter if you are young or old, short or tall, able-bodied or disabled, archery is a fun way to fulfil your potential, whether that's as someone who just enjoys shooting or as a future Olympian or Paralympian.

This book is intended to guide you on your first steps. It will tell you all about the different types of archery, what equipment you will need, what to expect when you start shooting and entering competitions, the basics of technique and how to stay safe. It's also great for people coming back to the sport after a break because it is packed with useful tips and reminders.

Whether you're a beginner or coming back, there's lots of support out there. There is a network of clubs across the UK ready to give you a warm welcome and help you become a better archer. They are all part of Archery GB, the UK sport's governing body. Its main aim is to help clubs and coaches develop so they, in turn, can help all archers, from beginners to the elite, reach their full potential. You can find more details at www.archerygb.org – but more of that later. It's time to take that first step...

There are several types of archery practised in the UK. The main ones are target, field, clout and flight and each requires slightly different shooting methods and equipment.

Target archery

Target archery is the kind of archery shot at the Olympics and is the version most beginners learn first. It can take place either indoors or outdoors. Archers shoot a set number of arrows at targets which are set at specified distances on a flat surface.

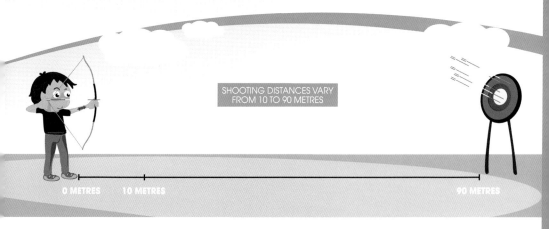

SHOOTING DISTANCES VARY
FROM 10 TO 90 METRES

0 METRES   10 METRES   90 METRES

Field archery

A field archery course is set up over woodland and rough terrain. Archers shoot a specified number of arrows at different targets in sequence. Archers might have to shoot uphill or downhill and the targets could be different sizes and at different distances, so anyone taking part has to really think about what they are doing.

FIELD ARCHERS
SHOOT AT A VARIETY
OF DISTANCES OVER
CHALLENGING TERRAIN

Clout shooting

This ancient form of archery was used as military training in the middle ages. The target is the clout, which is a small flag on a vertical stick, stuck in the ground and placed up to 165 metres away. An archer's score is determined by how close each arrow lands to the flag. The scores are measured by a tape attached to the flag and the arrows that land closest get the highest points.

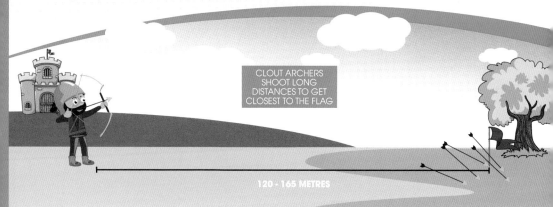

CLOUT ARCHERS SHOOT LONG DISTANCES TO GET CLOSEST TO THE FLAG

120 - 165 METRES

Flight shooting

This form of archery is simply shooting an arrow over the longest possible distance. It requires a very large flat area – about the size of an aerodrome. Recurve, compound and longbow classes can all shoot within different weight categories. Specialist bows and arrows are also used to maximise power and reduce drag.

Archers can shoot distances of 270 metres with a longbow and 900 metres with a compound flight bow.

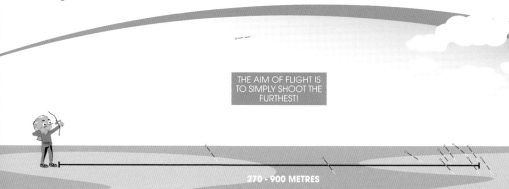

THE AIM OF FLIGHT IS TO SIMPLY SHOOT THE FURTHEST!

270 - 900 METRES

If you are going to shoot you need to know what equipment you will need, how it works - and how to use it safely.

THE ARCHERY FOR BEGINNERS GUIDEBOOK

Equipment

Like most sports, archery can involve a large range of equipment and accessories. But you only really need basic equipment to get started - a bow, some arrows, a bracer, finger tab, a quiver and a target to shoot at.

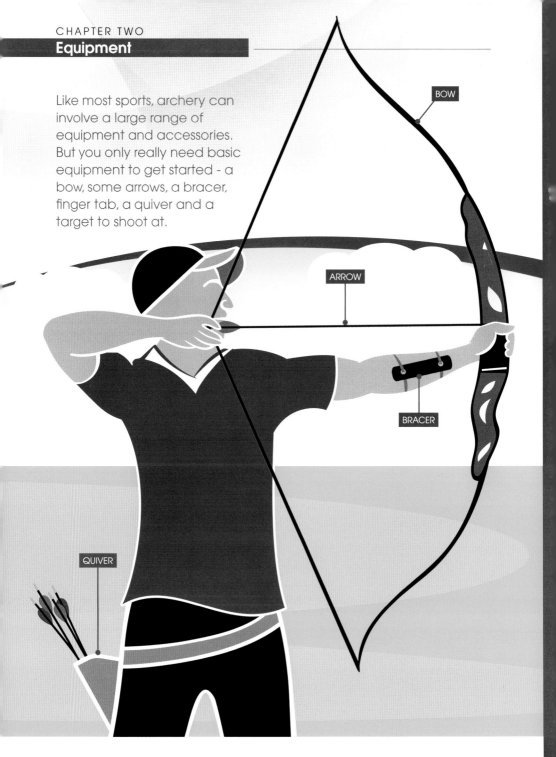

BOW

ARROW

BRACER

QUIVER

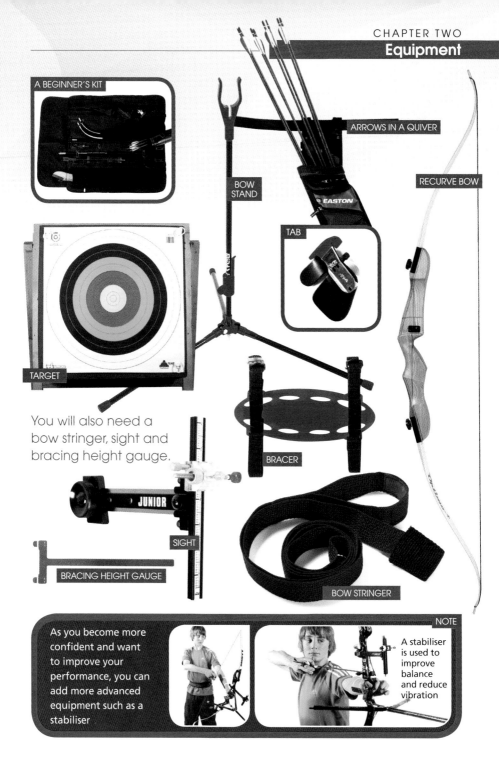

A BEGINNER'S KIT

ARROWS IN A QUIVER

BOW STAND

RECURVE BOW

TAB

TARGET

You will also need a bow stringer, sight and bracing height gauge.

BRACER

JUNIOR

SIGHT

BRACING HEIGHT GAUGE

BOW STRINGER

NOTE

As you become more confident and want to improve your performance, you can add more advanced equipment such as a stabiliser

A stabiliser is used to improve balance and reduce vibration

Types of bow

There are three main types of bow: recurve, compound and longbow.

Recurve bow

The recurve bow is usually used to introduce beginners to archery.

It is designed so the limb tips curve away from the archer, and stores more energy than a straight-limbed bow.

As recurve archers become experienced, they add more pieces of equipment to their bows, such as stabilisers to help with balance and absorb some of the vibration, sights to improve accuracy and pressure buttons to fine tune the arrow's flight.

Compound bow

A compound bow is a modern bow which provides maximum performance. Its handle is similar to the recurve bow, but has very short, powerful limbs that are attached to pulley wheels and cables used to draw the limbs back.

Longbow

The longbow is a traditional bow and holds huge historical significance. Longbows are hand crafted from a variety of different woods, including yew, lemonwood and hickory, or from just a single piece. Longbows are less accurate and are more difficult to shoot than modern bow designs - but people who shoot them say that this makes them much more fun.

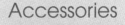

COMPOUND BOW

RECURVE BOW

LONGBOW

Accessories

Quiver

A side quiver is attached to a belt around the waist and holds arrows while you are shooting.

A ground quiver is placed on or into the ground to hold bows and arrows.

Bow stand

A simple metal stand used to hold a bow.

Bracer

A bracer is used to keep loose clothing from touching the string and stop the string hitting the arm, which can cause bruising.

The bracer is fitted to the inside of the arm holding the bow, between the elbow joint and the wrist. The widest end of the bracer fits closest to the elbow.

Finger tab

A tab provides protection for the fingers that draw the string.

Bow stringer

A bow stringer is used to string and unstring a bow. For your own safety it is always best to learn to do this under the guidance of an experienced archer or coach.

Bracing height gauge

The brace height is the distance between the deepest part of the handle and the bow string. A bracing height gauge is used to measure the point where the arrow should be clipped on to the bow string. Get the height right because, if it is too low or too high, the bow will shoot erratically.

Recurve bow

This bow is usually used to introduce beginners to archery.

UPPER LIMB

BOW STRING

RISER

LOWER LIMB

Getting it right when choosing a bow is crucial, so you will need help in the early stages

You need to feel comfortable with your bow to make sure you get the maximum fun and satisfaction. Getting it wrong could result in frustration and injury – so talk to a coach or retail specialist for guidance

Most recurve bows are 'take-down' bows. This means that the limbs can be detached from the riser, as shown in the picture, to make it easier to transport and store.

Beginner bows usually have 'limbs' which are made of laminated wood and flat fibreglass strips. Right handed and left handed bows are available.

A recurve bow is made up of:

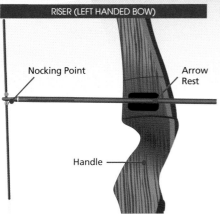

RISER (LEFT HANDED BOW)

Nocking Point

Arrow Rest

Handle

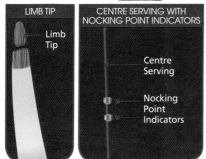

LIMB TIP

Limb Tip

CENTRE SERVING WITH NOCKING POINT INDICATORS

Centre Serving

Nocking Point Indicators

Riser: The centre section of a bow. It includes the handle and arrow rest.

- Handle: The part of the riser held by the bow hand.

- Arrow rest: An arrow rest is a simple device that fits to the riser of the bow to hold the arrow in the correct position when it is being shot. It is flexible enough not to interfere with the arrow's flight.

Limb (upper and lower): The 'working' part of the bow. It bends when the bow is drawn.

- Limb tip: The very end of a bow limb, which includes a groove for the string.

Bow string: The cord running between the limb tips which bends the bow.

- Centre serving: Reinforced area on the bow string where the arrow and fingers are placed.

- Nocking point indicators: Small guides on the centre serving of the bow string used to mark the point (the 'nock') where you click the arrow on to the string.

Arrows

An arrow is made up of different components:

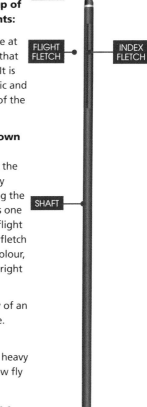

NOCK

FLIGHT FLETCH

INDEX FLETCH

SHAFT

PILE

Nock: A plastic groove at the end of the arrow that clips on to the string. It is made from rigid plastic and attaches to the shaft of the arrow.

Fletchings - also known as vanes:
Plastic attachments at the end of the arrow. They provide stability during the arrow's flight. There is one index fletch and two flight fletchings. (The index fletch is usually a different colour, to help you put it the right way on the string).

Shaft: The main body of an arrow is a hollow tube.

Pile: The point of the arrow. It is made with heavy metal to help the arrow fly straight.

Arrows are available in a variety of sizes and quality,

and made from either aluminium or carbon fibre – or both. Aluminium arrows are the toughest and widely used by beginners and club archers.

> **NOTE**
>
> Make sure that you use an arrow that is the correct length for you
>
> Using an arrow that is too short can damage your bow or, even worse, cause serious injuries

Target

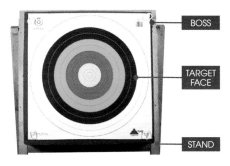

BOSS

TARGET FACE

STAND

A target is made up of:

Boss: Designed to stop arrows safely, made from tightly packed foam or wound straw. Bosses are placed on a stand, leaning back at a 15 degree angle.

Target face: Made with reinforced paper and pinned to the boss.

Stand: Used to hold in place and elevate the boss.

Identify damaged equipment

Always check your equipment for damage before it is used.

It is usual for archers to maintain their own equipment. This includes fitting an arrow rest, attaching nocking point indicators, and fitting an arrow nock.

> **NOTE**
>
> Store your equipment indoors in a cool, dry place.
>
> Any equipment found to be damaged should not be used until the defect is repaired or replaced

Ask an experienced archer, coach or retailer for guidance before you attempt to make any adjustments yourself.

Many clubs hold workshops to teach their members about basic maintenance.

Here are some typical types of damage that you should check for.

Bow:

- Cracked or delaminated limbs
- Worn limb tips
- Worn, missing or loose arrows rest
- Twisted or damaged limbs

LYONS

Bowstring:

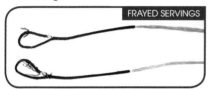

- Frayed strands
- Loose or frayed centre serving
- Nocking point positioned incorrectly (e.g. the gap is too large)

Arrow:

The shaft should be straight, smooth and without any kinks. You can check for any wobbles or bends by rolling the arrow on a flat surface or spinning the arrow on your hand. Check for:

- Missing, broken or loose fletchings
- Damaged pile and nock
- Shaft that is bent or damaged

Hand dominance

As soon as you pick up a bow and draw back the string you will know what feels most comfortable.

You can get both right and left-handed bows. A right-handed bow is held in the left hand, and the string is drawn using the right hand. If you are right handed you will probably feel more comfortable with a right-handed bow. But there are other factors too.

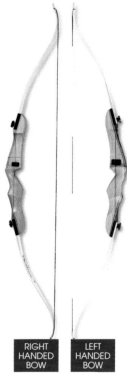

Eye dominance

Archers rely on the use of a single eye to aim. This 'aiming eye' is used to line up the arrow with the target.

Everyone has a natural tendency to rely on one eye rather the other. This is known as the 'dominant eye'.

To aim correctly, ideally the dominant eye and the hand with which you draw the string should match.

For example, someone who is right hand dominant (draws the string with their right hand) should aim using his or her right eye.

Check which is your dominant eye:

1. Extend both hands in front of you, and overlay them leaving a small gap.
2. Keep both of your eyes open and look through the gap at a fixed point
3. Draw your hands back close to your face keeping your gaze on the fixed point
4. Your hand will lead you to your dominant eye

When hand and eye dominance don't match

Sometimes an archer's dominant eye and dominant hand are not the same.

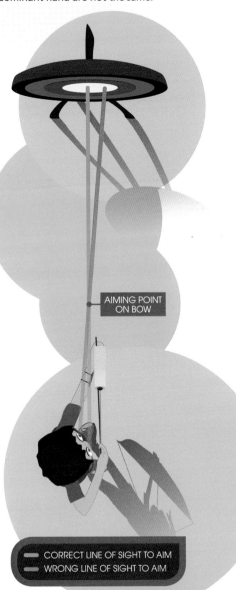

AIMING POINT ON BOW

CORRECT LINE OF SIGHT TO AIM
WRONG LINE OF SIGHT TO AIM

For example, if an archer draws the string with their right hand (right handed) but their left eye is dominant, it can cause problems lining up the arrow with the target.

When this happens the archer can either:

- Cover the dominant eye and aim with the eye that matches the dominant hand
- Change bows, so that the dominant eye and hand now match

How to select a bow and arrow

Every archer needs slightly different equipment. It depends on which hand they shoot with, their size and their physical capacity.

These simple steps will help you to make the right choice.

> **NOTE**
> Use a qualified coach to guide you through your first archery experiences and to provide you with the appropriate equipment

Select an arrow

Choosing the right arrow is vital. You must never use an arrow that is too short because when you draw it, it can fall off the arrow rest and damage the bow. Even worse, it can seriously damage you.

How to check safe arrow length

1 Place your thumb on your nose and fully extend your other arm to the side, with your hand pointing upwards

2 Place the arrow nock in the 'V' of the palm next to your face, and rest the shaft against the 'V' of your outstretched hand

MAKE SURE THAT YOU ASK A COACH TO SELECT ARROWS THAT ARE SAFE AND SUITABLE FOR YOU

✓ This arrow is the right length

IF YOU CANNOT FIND AN ARROW THAT IS LONG ENOUGH, YOU MUST NOT SHOOT

✗ The arrow is too short

1 Decide if you need a left or right handed bow

3 Use a bow of the correct length and draw weight

2 Fit your bracer and finger tab

4 Select arrows that are long enough for you

3 A correct sized arrow will extend at least two inches past the 'V' of the outstretched hand. If it does not, you need a longer arrow

4 If you cannot find an arrow that is long enough, **YOU MUST NOT SHOOT**. Never shoot with a short arrow, or hold the bow bending your arm to compensate

Select a bow

There are three things to remember when choosing a suitable bow:

Do you need a right or left-handed bow?

What bow length do you need?

What draw weight do you need?

1. Right and left handed bows

Decide which hand you prefer to use. Remember, it might depend on eye dominance.

- A right-handed bow is one that is drawn with the right hand and held in the left.
- A left-handed bow is one that is drawn with the left hand and held in the right.

2. Bow length

It is important for you to use a bow that is the correct size for you. This will give you a comfortable finger position on the string, which will help you shoot accurately.

Too short: Using a bow that is too short will make the limbs of the bow bend too much. In extreme cases, this could cause the arrow to fall off the arrow rest at full draw

Too long: Using a bow that is too long will stop the limbs of the bow bending enough at full draw – and that means less power to propel the arrow.

DIFFERENT SIZE BOWS

NOTE

Labelling on a bow

The bow length and draw weight is usually marked on the bottom limb of the bow

LONGSHOT TD-01 TRAINER

Bow length is measured in inches (") and draw weight is measured in pounds (lbs)

A '70/22' bow. The bow length is 70 inches and draw weight is 22lbs

3. Draw weight

Draw weight is the force needed to draw back the bow string. A bow with a high draw weight will feel harder to pull than one with a low draw weight.

NOTE

Draw weight is also known as 'poundage' as it is measured in pounds (lbs)

It is important to make sure your bow has the right draw weight for your size, age and physical capacity. You only need a bow powerful enough to hit the target at the distance being shot. The draw weight should be low enough so that you can draw and hold the bow comfortably, without any strain or discomfort. This will help cut the risk of injuring your muscles and help you develop a good shooting technique.

String a bow

A bow stringer is used to string and unstring a recurve bow to prevent injury and protect the bow.

Bows need to be unstrung when they are being stored to stop the limbs being damaged.

SADDLE AND POUCH

> **NOTE**
> For your own safety, make sure you learn to string a bow under the guidance of a coach

A bow stringer has two parts. On one end is called the saddle and on the other end the pouch. The saddle is fitted to the top limb of the bow and the pouch is fitted to the bottom limb.

How to string a bow

1. Loosely attach the bowstring

Pass the top (big) loop of the bowstring over the top limb, and slide it along a few centimeters past the tip.

Put the bottom (small) loop over the bottom limb tip and secure the string into the groove.

2. Fit the saddle and pouch

Place the saddle on to the top limb and then secure the pouch on to the bottom limb tip.

3. Position your hands and feet

Both ends of the stringer will now be in place. Support the saddle with a thumb or finger and place one foot fully over the cord of the stringer.

4. Fix the string on to the upper limb

Safety first! Make sure your head is well above the point where the limbs attach to the riser (the limb pocket).

Push the saddle as close to the end of the limb as the string loop will allow. Pull on bow handle, while the other hand supports the saddle. This will flex the limbs of the bow. Slide the top loop of the string into the notches of the top limb tip, so that the string lies in the groove at the back.

5. Relax the bow

Relax the bow by relaxing your pull against the bow handle. The bow should now be strung. Remove the bow stringer and check that each string loop is correctly positioned in the grooves of the limb tip.

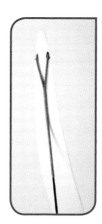

> **NOTE**
>
> **Caution:** When relaxing the bow there is a chance the saddle might slip, causing the top limb to 'spring' upwards. If your face is too close, there is a danger it could be hit. Always make sure your face is well away from the limb tip and support the saddle against the limb

How to destring a bow

1. Fit the saddle and pouch

Place the saddle over the top limb, and the pouch on the bottom limb tip.

2. Position your hands and feet

Both ends of the stringer will now be in place. Support the saddle with a thumb or finger and place one foot fully over the cord of the stringer.

3. Remove the top string from the top limb

Make sure your head is above the limb pocket of the riser. Pull on the bow handle and support the saddle with the other hand. This will flex the limbs of the bow. Slide the top loop of the bowstring off the top limb tip and a few centimeters along.

4. Relax the bow

Relax the bow limbs by relaxing your pull against the bow handle. The bow should now be unstrung and the string can safely be removed.

> **NOTE**
>
> **Caution:** If you have been shooting in the rain and your bow is wet, dry the bow limbs carefully before attempting to de-string the bow

Archers rely on the use of a single eye to aim. This 'aiming eye' is used to line up the arrow with the target

Adjust bracing height

Bracing height is the distance between the bowstring and the pressure button hole. (If the bow doesn't have a pressure button hole, the deepest part of the handle can be used as a reference point).

A bracing height that is either too low or too high will cause the bow to perform erratically. The bow will perform better if it is set correctly.

Check the bracing height once the bow is strung.

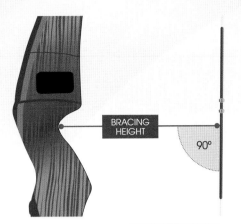

BRACING HEIGHT

90°

How to measure bracing height

Bracing height is measured with a bracing height gauge. The bracing height gauge has markings along its length in either inches or millimetres.

Clip the gauge to the string and read the distance from the string to the pressure button hole.

Follow the bow manufacturer's guidance to set the bracing height. If the bracing height is outside of the recommended range then it can be raised or lowered by partially de-stringing the bow, adding or taking away twists to the string and then restringing it.

Target archery takes place on a marked out area known as a range.

CHAPTER THREE
The Range

Range layout

A range can be indoors or outdoors but it needs to be carefully set out and managed to make sure everyone – the archers, spectators and passers-by are kept safe at all times.

Safety is the key to an archery range which is why there is a special layout and strict rules about discipline and behaviour.

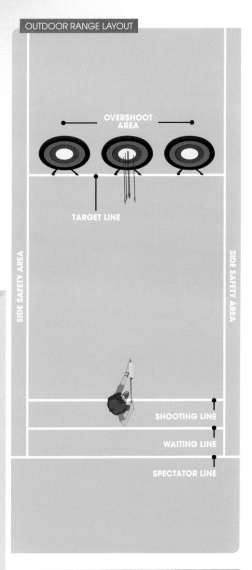

OUTDOOR RANGE LAYOUT

OVERSHOOT AREA

TARGET LINE

SIDE SAFETY AREA

SIDE SAFETY AREA

SHOOTING LINE

WAITING LINE

SPECTATOR LINE

INDOOR RANGE LAYOUT

BACKSTOP NETTING

TARGET LINE

SHOOTING LINE

WAITING LINE

NOTE

Rules of Shooting

For full guidance on range layout and range distances download the Rules of Shooting from www.archerygb.org

Overshoot area:

An area behind the targets on an outdoor range. It is cordoned off for safety.

If the range is indoors, it is an area behind the backstop netting.

Side safety area:

An area on an outdoor range that runs down the side of the targets. It is also cordoned off for safety.

Target line:

An identified distance at which targets are set down and secured.

Shooting line:

A visible line on the ground from which archers shoot at the targets. You can only shoot from this line.

Waiting line:

A visible line on the ground behind which archers must wait before they begin shooting.

Spectator line:

An area behind the shooting line for the people who are watching and not taking part.

The basic rules

These basic rules have to be followed at all times to make sure everybody stays safe:

- During shooting the field of play has to be free of people, pets, and obstacles.
- Archers only load and shoot their arrows standing at the shooting line. There is only one shooting line for all archers.

- Shooting only takes place at designated times and the archer may not load an arrow into the bow until the signal to start shooting is given.
- Archers shoot only at the target which corresponds to their place on the shooting line.
- Shooting is in one direction only.
- Archers aim continuously toward their target when drawing their bow. The bow must not be drawn in such away that if the string was accidentally released the arrow would fly out of the safety zone.
- On all ranges the whole shooting range needs to be marked off, with warning signs that archery is in progress facing outwards on the boundaries and all potential access points.

Safety procedures

Archers must never:

- Direct the bow at anyone or anything other than the target
- Release the string without an arrow ('dry shoot') as it damages the bow
- Shoot upwards into the air
- Step over the shooting line to retrieve an arrow that has dropped from the bow
- Run on the range

Archers must always:

- Stay behind the waiting line until a command is given to start shooting
- Only load or shoot a bow from the shooting line
- Only direct a loaded bow towards the target
- Return to the waiting line after they have finished shooting
- Stay behind the waiting line until a command is given to collect the arrows
- Move to the targets at a calm walking speed and as a single group to collect arrows

NO ENTRY
Archery In Progress

ON THE ARCHERY RANGE, SAFETY AND SHOOTING PROCEDURES ARE UNDER THE CONTROL OF ONE PERSON, USUALLY REFERRED TO AS A FIELD CAPTAIN OR RANGE SAFETY OFFICER

Range commands

The field captain will explain to all archers what commands will be used on the range to manage safety and behaviour. These can be verbal commands or blasts on a whistle. The most important commands are listed below:

Command	What it means	When it is used
GO or COMMENCE SHOOTING	This permits archers to move from the waiting line to the shooting line and commence shooting	This is the main means of safety control on the shooting range and is used at every end of arrows
COLLECT	This permits the archers to move over the shooting line and go to the targets to retrieve arrows	This command is used at every end of arrows
STOP or FAST	This means stop immediately. Participants must come down if at full draw, remove the arrow from the bow, return to the waiting line and wait for the command to start shooting again	Anyone can use this command when there is any perceived hazard. For example: • A person or dog on the range • A hanging arrow in a target
COME DOWN	The command is directed to participants on an individual basis. The participant should bring the bow down to relaxed position	Coaches use this when working with an archer, for example to: • Start the shot again • Make an adjustment to technique or equipment

The way archers position themselves to shoot an arrow is known as their technique – and not all archers use the same technique. But there are common techniques that archers need to know to give themselves a good foundation so they can progress.

CHAPTER FOUR

Technique

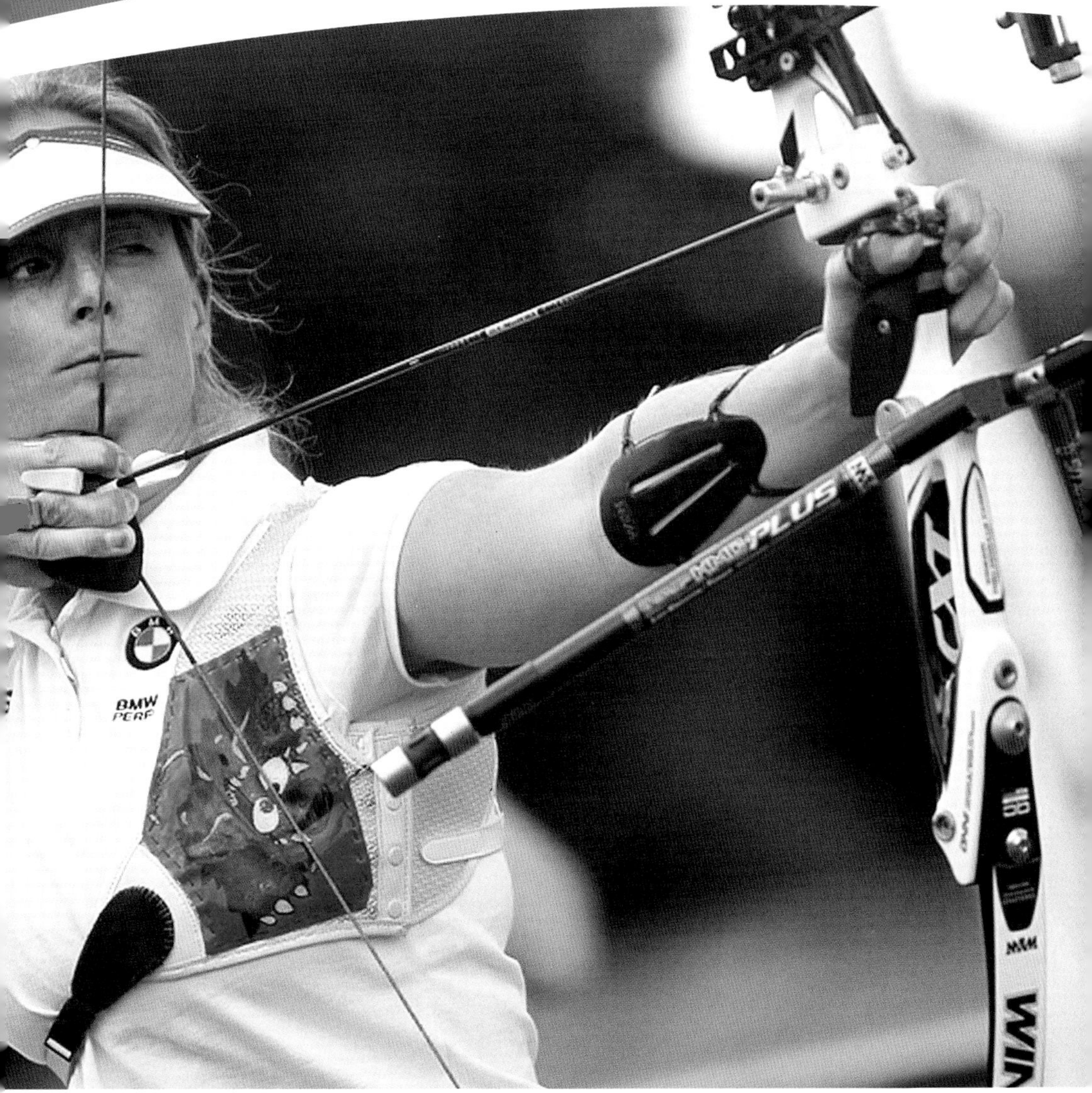

T-Draw shooting

T-Draw shooting technique teaches core skills that will help you progress, refine technique to a high standard and reduce the risk of injury.

The fundamental steps of T-Draw shooting technique are:

STANCE

NOCK THE ARROW

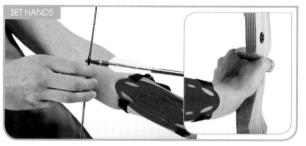

SET HANDS

PREPARE

RAISE

DRAW

ANCHOR AND AIM

RELEASE

Understand posture

Posture provides the foundation of shooting technique. Good posture will help you shoot better.

By using T-Draw shooting technique, the body forms a solidly balanced 'T' shape with two important features:

1. Vertical posture. Starts in the 'prepare' step. You hold it until the shot is complete.

2. Level shoulders and arms. Starts in the 'raise' step. You hold it until the shot is complete.

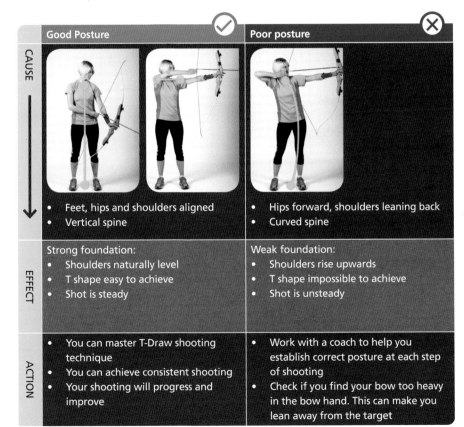

	Good Posture ✓	Poor posture ✗
CAUSE	• Feet, hips and shoulders aligned • Vertical spine	• Hips forward, shoulders leaning back • Curved spine
EFFECT	Strong foundation: • Shoulders naturally level • T shape easy to achieve • Shot is steady	Weak foundation: • Shoulders rise upwards • T shape impossible to achieve • Shot is unsteady
ACTION	• You can master T-Draw shooting technique • You can achieve consistent shooting • Your shooting will progress and improve	• Work with a coach to help you establish correct posture at each step of shooting • Check if you find your bow too heavy in the bow hand. This can make you lean away from the target

Barebow and Freestyle shooting styles

Barebow and Freestyle are two types of shooting style that follow the steps of the T-Draw technique.

- Barebow involves an archer shooting a bow with no attachments

- Freestyle involves the archer shooting with extra attachments, such as a sight

- There are three main differences between shooting barebow and freestyle

A SIGHT USED IN FREESTYLE SHOOTING

T-Draw technique: Barebow

Place three fingers on the string below the arrow

'Anchor' the draw hand against the corner of your mouth

Use the point of the arrow to aim

T-Draw technique: Freestyle

Place three fingers on the string, one above the arrow and two below

'Anchor' the draw hand underneath your jaw

Use a sight to aim

Barebow

1. Stance	2. Nock the arrow	3. Set hands	4. Prepare

• Relax and take a breath • Line up your feet • Prepare your stance	• Load the arrow on to the bow	• Hook the fingers of your drawing hand on to the string • Position your bow hand on the handle	• Focus on the target • Achieve the 'preparation line'

5. Raise	6. Draw	7. Anchor and aim	8. Release

• Look at the target • Raise your arms to the height of your nose • Balance 'push and pull'	• Focus on the target • Draw the bow • Hold at full draw • Achieve the 'draw force line'	• Anchor your draw hand so the index finger touches corner of your mouth • Aim the point of the arrow • The push and pull at full draw helps keep the bow steady	• Relax your draw hand to release the string • Focus on the target • Maintain your posture and keep your head still

Freestyle

1. Stance	2. Nock the arrow	3. Set hands	4. Prepare

• Relax and take a breath • Line up your feet • Prepare your stance	• Load the arrow on to the bow	• Hook the fingers of your drawing hand on to the string • Position your bow hand on the handle	• Focus on the target • Achieve the 'preparation line'

5. Raise	6. Draw	7. Anchor and aim	8. Release

• Focus on the target • Raise your arms to the height of your nose • Balance 'push and pull'	• Focus on the target • Draw the bow • Hold at full draw • Achieve the 'draw force line'	• Anchor your draw hand under the jaw with the string touching your chin and nose • Aim the arrow using the sight	• Relax your draw hand • Focus on the target • Maintain your posture and keep your head still

Improvements to technique

There are common ways that you can improve T-Draw shooting technique.

1. Stance: Stand side-on to the target

Stance affects the direction of the body and the direction of aiming towards the target. If your feet are in different positions for different shots, you will struggle to shoot consistently.

What to do

- Stand with feet shoulder width apart, side on to the target
- Look forward along the shooting line

SHOOTING LINE

DIRECTION TO TARGET

HINT
Beginners often forget to check their feet before starting to shoot so practise your stance to position your body correctly for the shot

- Lay an arrow across the shooting line pointing towards the target
- Line your toes up with the arrow
- You have now found the ideal position for your feet

2. Nock the arrow: Listen for the click

Listen and feel for the 'click' when you nock the arrow. If the nock doesn't fit the bow string then it will not click into place.

What to do

- Hold the bow with a relaxed arm
- Take an arrow and place it on to the arrow rest
- Click the nock of the arrow on to the bow string
- Ensure that the index fletching is positioned away from the bow

FEEL FOR THE CLICK

INDEX FLETCHING POINTS OUTWARDS

HINT
Point the arrow towards the targets at all times

Pick the arrow up by the nock to avoid damaging the vanes

3. Set hands: Set your bow hand and hook your fingers

Bow hand position

What to do

- Place your hand against the bow handle
- Line up the base of the thumb to push against the handle
- Relax the hand

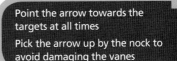

Hook your fingers

Placing the draw fingers on to the string is known as 'hooking'. The only difference between Barebow and Freestyle hooking is the position of the fingers on the string. Everything else remains the same.

What to do

- The string is lined up close to the first joint of the fingers

- Place the fingers on the string in the same position for every shot to achieve consistency

- Keep the bow hand relaxed and the back of the hand flat while the fingers are hooked

- The string should contact each finger on the first finger crease

- A hooking position that is either too deep or too shallow will make the release difficult

- If fingers are placed too close to the arrow, they can press on the arrow. This will affect the way the arrow flies upon release and is likely to send it off target

- Don't hold or pinch the back of the arrow

Barebow

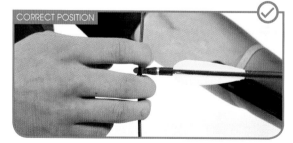

CORRECT POSITION

All three fingers placed underneath the arrow

CORRECT HOOK

DEEP HOOK

SHALLOW HOOK

PINCHING

Freestyle

CORRECT POSITION

One finger placed above the arrow and two underneath

CORRECT HOOK

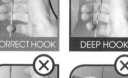
DEEP HOOK

SHALLOW HOOK

SQUEEZING

THE ARCHERY FOR BEGINNERS GUIDEBOOK

Stance affects the direction of the body and the direction of aiming towards the target. If your feet are in different positions for different shots, you will struggle to shoot consistently

4. Prepare: Achieve the 'preparation line' and consistent posture

The preparation line:

Hold the bow so there is a straight line from the elbow of the drawing arm, through where your fingers are holding the string, to where your hand is placed in the bow handle. This is called the 'preparation line'.

What to do

Balance bow hand and hook:
- As the bow hand is placed against the handle, apply a light push with the bow arm and a light pull on the string.
- This needs to feel like a balanced force in either direction

THE PREPARATION LINE: A STRAIGHT IMAGINARY LINE FROM ELBOW, FINGERS TO BOW HAND

PRACTISE ACHIEVING THIS POSITION WITH AND WITHOUT A BOW

Breathe:
- Take a deep breath in and let it out slowly, helping to relax

Posture check:
- Check that posture is stable, upright and balanced

Focus:
- Turn your head towards the target, keep it still
- Look at your aiming point on the target
- Block out any distractions around you

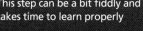

HINT

This step can be a bit fiddly and takes time to learn properly

- Start off by practising the routine without a bow
- Next practise with a bow but without an arrow
- This will help you gain confidence and understand the sequence of steps

Common errors

Rushing:
- Try not to rush this step. Focusing on the breath is useful for relaxation and slowing down.

Drawing too early:
- Try not to over emphasise the balance between bow hand and draw hand. You need a light and balanced push and pull, the string should only move back about 1-2 inches at this stage.

Posture:

Posture is the key to archery technique. It needs to be safe, comfortable – and consistent.

How does effective posture help?

- It provides a stable platform to shoot the bow
- It ensures body weight is evenly spread between both feet
- It is comfortable and easy to reproduce
- It suits the individual

What to do

Maintain the following position:
- Feet, hips and shoulders lined up
- A vertical spine
- Knees relaxed

CORRECT POSTURE

> HINT
> - Link the idea of good posture with a letter 'T'
> - Practise making a 'T' shape with your arms out to the side
> - Link the 'T' shape to good posture while shooting
> - Draw a bow without an arrow so you think only about posture and are not distracted by having to shoot an arrow

Common errors

Arched back
- Unstable and difficult to replicate
- May lead to lower back injuries

Possible reasons:
- Leaning forward
- Moving head forward to string

ARCHED BACK

- Not drawing the string far enough back
- Not standing up straight before raising bow arm

Hollow back
- Unstable and difficult to replicate
- May lead to reduced string clearance across chest
- Often accompanied by a high bow shoulder and string hitting the bow arm

Possible reasons:
- Pelvis not tucked in

HOLLOW BACK

5. Raise: Maintain the 'preparation line'

The bow arm and draw arm should be raised together as one unit to a position where both hands are about level with the nose. This step gets the arms and shoulders in the right position to start the draw.

What to do

- Raise both arms up together
- Both hands finish about level with your nose
- Shoulders remain in a natural, low and level position
- Posture remains upright and balanced
- Maintain the preparation line

> HINT
> - Raise both arms upwards to the height of your nose
> - Breathe in as you do this
> - Notice how at all times you keep a straight line between the draw elbow, string fingers and bow hand
> - Practise this step without a bow
> - Repeat with a bow
> - When the raise position is complete, keep a balanced push against the bow and pull against the string

Practise the raise without a bow

Practise the raise with a clini band

Practise the raise with bow

Common errors

Leaning:
Stay upright rather than lean away. Leaning might indicate that your bow is too heavy.

Hunching:
Shoulders should be kept relaxed and level, not hunched.

LEANING BACK

RELAXED SHOULDERS   HUNCHED SHOULDERS

Rushing:
The raise and draw are two separate movements. However, it is common for archers to rush and raise the bow and draw it at the same time.

To prevent this, practise getting into the 'T' shape, complete the raise, and then start the next step.

6. Draw: Bring the string back and achieve the 'draw force line'

The purpose of the draw is to store energy in the bow to shoot the arrow

What to do

- Ensure that the full draw position can be repeated for each shot
- Draw the string back towards your face
- Keep your shoulders relaxed and down
- The movement should be smooth and take 1-2 seconds.

Practise the draw without a bow

Practise the draw with a clini band

Practise the draw with a bow

- The action is aided by breathing out half a breath and keeping the balance of a push and pull
- Get a feel for the action and understand the steps

What to do
- Rest the draw hand in the appropriate position on your face (for either barebow or freestyle)
- This is the anchor position
- The back of the hand is flat and shows no sign of tension

Common errors

Hunching the shoulders:
If you are hunching your shoulders at pre-draw, it is likely they were hunched during the raise. You could be trying too hard. Don't tense up, relax and have fun!

Leaning on the toes:
It is common to find archers leaning on to their toes during the draw. This happens when they move their body towards the bow string. Stay relaxed and bring the draw arm straight back towards your face.

LEANING ON TOES

The 'draw force line'
The imaginary straight line that runs from the elbow, draw hand and bow hand at full draw is called the 'draw force line'.

The full draw position is the last step before the release.

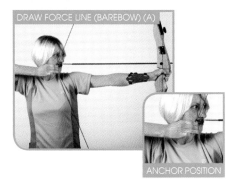

DRAW FORCE LINE (BAREBOW) (A)

ANCHOR POSITION

DRAW FORCE LINE (FREESTYLE) (B)

ANCHOR POSITION

Barebow (A)
- Touch the tip of the index finger against the reference point, the corner of the mouth.
- The back of the hand is flat and shows no sign of tension.

Freestyle (B)
- The draw hand rests underneath the jaw bone.
- The top of the index finger rests against the bone line.
- The string touches the tip of the nose, and the front side of the chin.
- The back of the hand is flat and shows no sign of tension.

To gain greater consistency when shooting:

- Keep the full draw position at the same length for each shot (bow hand to draw elbow)
- Keep your position by slightly pushing forwards and pulling backwards
- Place the arrow in the same position each time
- Ensure the draw hand is referenced in exactly the same place on the face each time

7. Anchor and aim: Direct the arrow

The purpose of aiming is to help direct an arrow towards a target such as the 'gold' of a target face.

Barebow

What to do

- Look along the arrow
- Line it up against the target face
- Trial and error to find the aiming position that directs the arrow into the gold

ORIGINAL AIM

WHERE ARROWS LANDED

ADJUST THE AIM

ARROWS WILL LAND MORE CENTRALLY

- Look at the arrow point
- Hold the anchor position to ensure a consistent amount of energy goes into an arrow for each shot
- Line the point against the gold and relax the hand to release the string
- Shoot at least three arrows
- If the group is not in the centre of the target, adjust the aim away from the group

Freestyle

What to do

- Look through the sight ring, focusing on the target face
- The sight ring appears 'blurred'

> **HINT**
> - Set the sight so the vertical distance from arrow rest to sight is equal to the distance between your chin and eye
> - Aim at the gold and shoot a group of arrows (three arrows shot separately)
> - If the group is off centre, move the sight towards the group

1. THE ARCHER AIMED AT THE GOLD, BUT THE GROUP LANDED TO THE RIGHT

Up and Right

Common error

- Archer focuses on sight
- Target appears 'blurred'

2. THE SIGHT WAS MOVED UP AND TO THE RIGHT

3. THE ARCHER AIMED AT THE GOLD AGAIN, AND THE GROUP LANDED CLOSER TO THE GOLD

8. Release: Relax the fingers to release the arrow

The release and follow through happens in a short space of time and results from the previous steps.

What to do

- With the draw hand in the anchor position, the archer relaxes the fingers
- As the fingers relax the string will release and project the arrow forwards
- Allow the draw hand to naturally drop backwards
- The position is held until the arrow hits the target

RELEASE POSITION (BAREBOW AND FREESTYLE)

> **HINT**
> The release and follow through involves:
> - The bow hand fingers relaxing
> - The string moving forward and releasing the arrow forwards
> - Maintaining the push and pull until the arrow hits the target
> - Holding posture until the arrow has hit the target

PRACTISE THE RELEASE WITH A CLINI BAND (FREESTYLE)

Common errors

Flicking the fingers open:
Lots of archers will flick open their fingers to release the string. This can disturb the string during the release knocking the arrow slightly off-course. Practise the pre-draw and draw steps with a relaxed draw hand.

Looking for the arrow:
It is tempting to look to see where the arrow has landed immediately after the release. This can disrupt the release so try to ignore the arrow until it has hit the target (and even then there's nothing you can do about it!)

Gap shooting

Gap shooting is where an archer aims at different positions on the target to compensate for incorrect arrow point of impact.

Once an archer is reasonably consistent, gap shooting can be used to improve aiming.

THE ARCHER AIMS AT THE GOLD BUT THE ARROWS LANDED AT '1 'O CLOCK'

THE ARCHER ADJUSTED AIM TO '7 O'CLOCK' AND CHANGED WHERE THE ARROWS LANDED

An arrow is aimed at the centre of the gold but it strikes elsewhere. The archer compensates for this by taking an imaginary line from where the arrow landed, through the centre of the gold, to the same distance at the other side of the gold. This will be their new aiming point.

Collect arrows

Safety procedures

Once everyone has shot and the shooting line is clear, the field captain (or range safety officer) will give a command to go to the targets to retrieve the arrows.

1. Place the nearest hand against the boss, to stop the boss moving as you pull

2. Place your hand over the arrow, then grasp the arrow close to the target and withdraw backwards along the line of the arrow

3. Always look behind before you pull an arrow

4. Withdraw arrow along its line of flight (don't pull directly upwards)

5. Place the arrow into the hand that is against the target, or directly into your quiver

6. Hold arrows near the point with the shafts tucked under the arm and piles towards the floor

How to collect arrows

Walk calmly. Never run

- Check if any arrows are hidden in the ground
- Collect any arrows leading up to the boss
- Never pick up arrows from the ground immediately in front of the boss (you could risk impaling yourself against arrows in the target)
- Always approach the target from the side (you could risk impaling yourself)
- Never twist the arrow when removing it from the boss

- Before moving the hand on the boss, check that the point of the arrow is still on the arrow. If it isn't and your hand is still on the boss, you have a good idea where to find it
- Pull one arrow at a time
- Return arrows to a quiver or hold arrows near the point with the shafts tucked under the arm and piles towards the floor (make sure the ends of the arrows are not gripped in the hand in case of a trip)

Hazards

You can hurt yourself or others by:
- Walking into the end of an arrow that's still in the target or ground
- Pulling the arrow from a target or the ground. Always check behind you to make sure there is nobody standing close enough to be hurt when you pull the arrow out
- Falling over while carrying the arrows

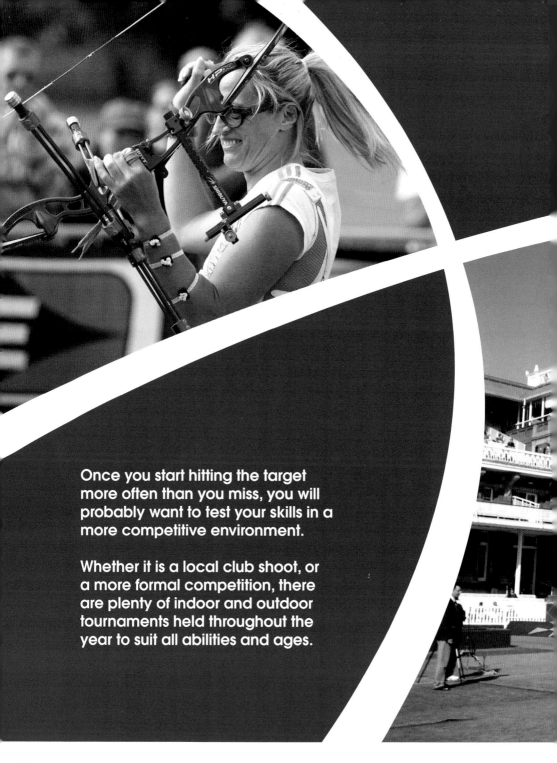

Once you start hitting the target more often than you miss, you will probably want to test your skills in a more competitive environment.

Whether it is a local club shoot, or a more formal competition, there are plenty of indoor and outdoor tournaments held throughout the year to suit all abilities and ages.

CHAPTER FIVE

Competitions

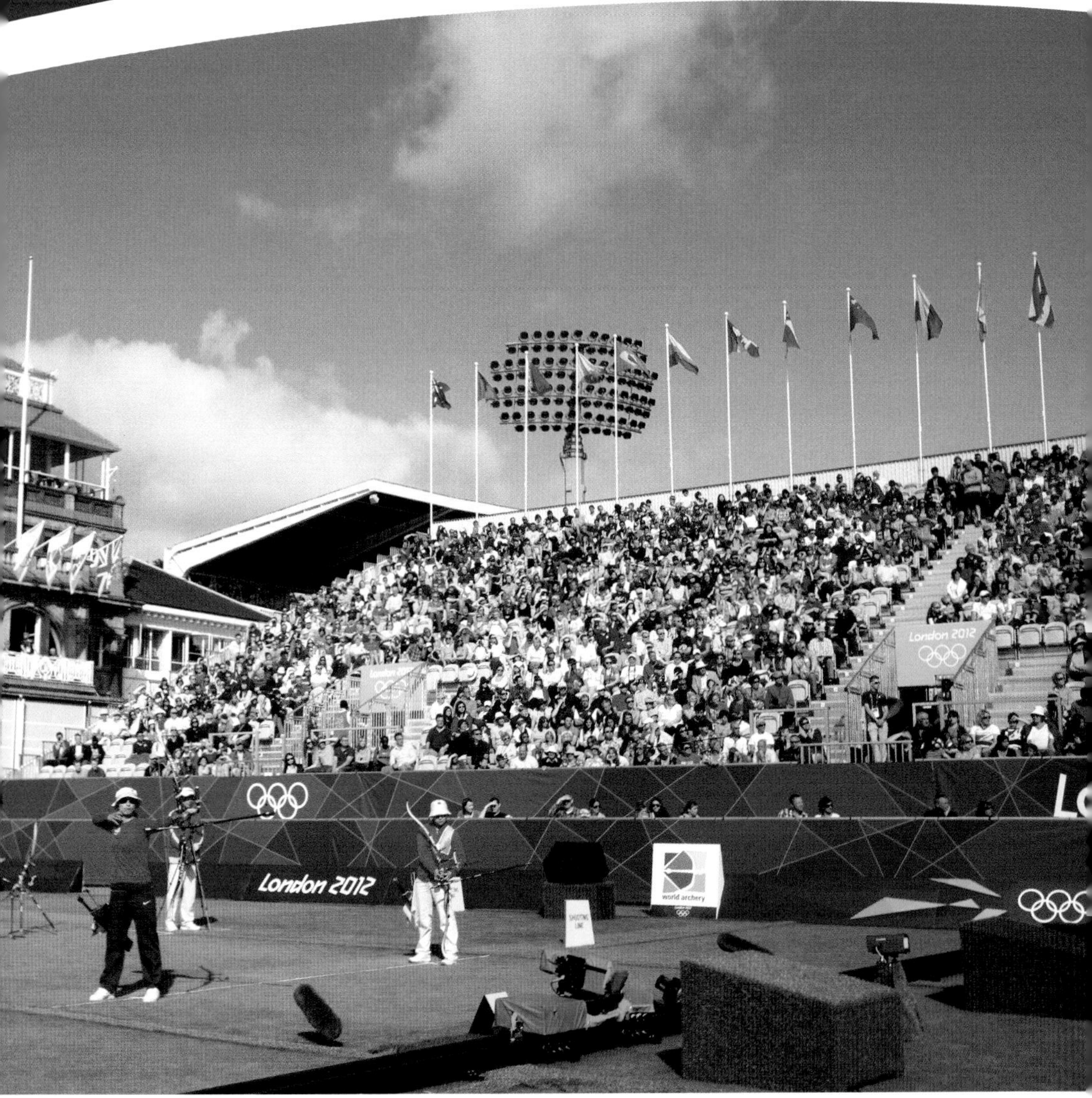

Competitions

Every archer remembers their first tournament. As well as helping you improve and compete, they are a great way to socialise, meet other archers and have fun. This chapter will guide you through your first target archery competition.

From beginner....

World Archery is the international governing body of archery. The World Archery Rules of Shooting can be downloaded from www.archery.org

Archery GB is the national governing body of archery in the UK and Northern Ireland. The Archery GB Rules of Shooting can be downloaded from www.archerygb.org

....To champion!

Scoring methods

In target archery there are two scoring methods, 5 Zone (Archery GB) and 10 Zone (World Archery). They use the same target face but have different scoring zones. In both any arrow touching a line separating zones (a 'line cutter'), scores the value of the higher scoring zone.

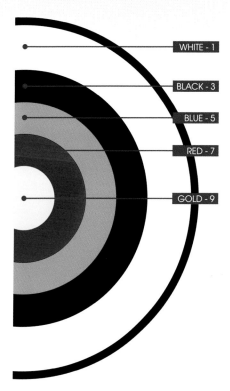

WHITE - 1
BLACK - 3
BLUE - 5
RED - 7
GOLD - 9

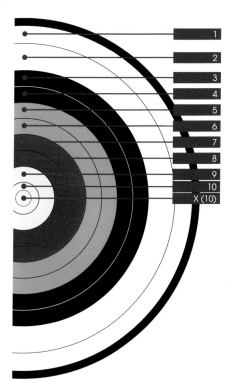

1
2
3
4
5
6
7
8
9
10
X (10)

5 Zone: Archery GB (imperial)

Scoring by colours
Archery GB rounds

The target is divided into 5 coloured scoring zones and points (9, 7, 5, 3, 1) are allocted depending on the colour the arrow lands in. This method is used for Archery GB rounds using imperial distances - measured in yards.

10 Zone: World Archery (metric)

Scoring by inner and outer rings
World Archery rounds

The target is divided into 10 scoring zones, each coloured area is split into two parts, the inner and outer ring. This method is used for World Archery rounds using metric distances - measured in metres - and for most indoor rounds.

Using a score sheet

Scores are recorded on a score sheet with the highest scoring arrow recorded first, for example "9-7-1". An arrow that does not score is called a miss and is marked 'M'.

Outdoor arrows are shot in 'ends' of six or three arrows (depending on the round or distance being shot). Once they have all been scored they can be removed from the target but the score sheet cannot be altered.

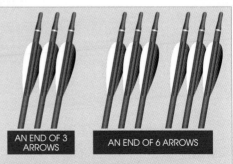

AN END OF 3 ARROWS

AN END OF 6 ARROWS

Indoor arrows are generally shot in groups of three and every six arrows shot are called an end.

				THE SCORES FOR EACH ARROW			TOTAL SCORE FROM 6 ARROWS		TWO ENDS ADDED TOGETHER			NUMBER OF ARROWS SCORING 10 IN WORLD ARCHERY OR 9 IN ARCHERY GB SCORING			
Name:															
			Score				End total		Score			End total	Score	Hits	Golds	Run Total
9	9	7	5	5	3	38		9	7	7	5	1 M 29	67	11	3	67
7	5	5	5	3	1	26		9	7	5	3	M M 24	50	10	1	117
9	7	7	5	5	5	38		9	9	7	7	5 5 42	80	12	3	197
Signed:								Date:							

(On World Archery Rounds, instead of 'hits' and 'golds' columns you will have '10s' and 'Xs' columns).

Rounds

Competition is organised so that you shoot a set number of arrows at specified distances and different sized target faces. This is known as a 'round'. For example:

A New Western round, shot at a 122cm target face, is:

- 4 dozen arrows at 100 yards
- and 4 dozen arrows at 80 yards

A Junior Western round, shot at a 122cm target face, is:

- 4 dozen arrows at 40 yards
- and 4 dozen arrows at 30 yards

FURTHER INFORMATION

Full details of all the rounds, distances, number of arrows and face size can be found in Archery GB's Rules of Shooting

Competitions

A Junior Western round

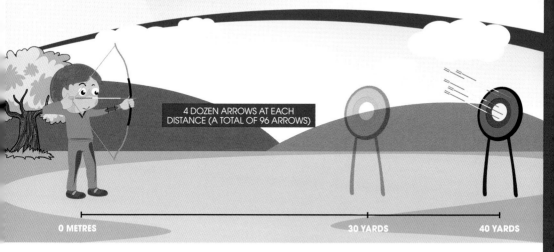

4 DOZEN ARROWS AT EACH DISTANCE (A TOTAL OF 96 ARROWS)

0 METRES   30 YARDS   40 YARDS

Archery GB Rounds (imperial): These tend to use five-zone scoring and are governed by the Archery GB Rules of Shooting. They commonly fall into 'families' – groups of different rounds held on the same field, at the same time, with the same number of arrows but at different distances. This means that you can choose the round that best suits your ability, age and gender.

You can choose whichever round you prefer. It does not matter if you shoot a round for a different age group or gender and adults can shoot a junior round (although they may not be eligible for any competition awards).

A TYPICAL SHOOTING LINE

Example family of rounds:

New Western   Short Western
Long Western   Junior Western
Western

World Archery rounds (metric): These are what you see at the Olympics and world championships. They are shot using the World Archery Rules of Shooting, and use 10-zone scoring and are a little more formal with stricter regulations and timings.

Indoor tournaments: At these events, everyone shoots the same distance.

THE USA TEAM CELEBRATE AT LONDON 2012

INDOOR TOURNAMENTS: AT THESE EVENTS, EVERYONE SHOOTS THE SAME DISTANCE

Levels of competition

Each round has a level or standard attached to it.

1. **World Record Status (WRS):** This is the highest level of competition and the most strictly controlled. Shooting in these tournaments gives you the opportunity to claim World, European and National Records as well as World Archery Target Awards. At least one National Judge will be present and controls can include traffic lights, whistles and occasionally countdown clocks to let you know when to shoot.

2. **UK Record Status (RS):** These can be either Archery GB or World Archery rounds and you might be able to shoot for national records or Rose Award status. At least one Regional Judge will be present.

3. **Non-Record Status (NRS):** These are relaxed tournaments where either Archery GB or World Archery rounds can be shot. Either a judge or an experienced archer will be in charge.

Finding a tournament

Members of Archery GB or World Archery can enter a World Record Status, National Record Status or Non-Record Status tournament.

Most clubs will have a notice board advertising local competitions.

All World and National Record Status tournaments are in the tournament diary on the Archery GB website and listed in the Archery UK magazine.

Other places to look are on regional, county and club archery websites.

Once you have chosen your tournament, complete the entry form and send it with your tournament fee to the organiser. Clubs often enter members into tournaments en masse but it is up to you to check what level or status the tournament is, the start time and location.

Preparing for the tournament

Packing for a competition can be a bit like packing for a holiday, so here are some handy tips:

As well as your bow and stand, make sure you take at least eight arrows – just in case you need spares. They must all be nocked and fletched in the same way and must have your name or initials on the shaft to identify them.

It is always a good idea to take some other spares too. The top archers always have a spare bow – but you will be fine with some spare nocks, a string and tab and a towel to wipe your equipment if it rains.

You will also need a pen for scoring, a calculator, an arrow puller and a score pad. There is a large range of apps available to help you score.

Spare Allen keys are a good idea, as are other bits like screwdrivers, spare fletchings, glue, scissors, pliers and binoculars for when you start shooting long distances. And remember you might need anything from a hat, sunscreen and sunglasses to an umbrella and wet weather gear – plus food and water. It's really important to keep well hydrated.

For Record Status events you have to follow dress regulations as set out in the Rules of Shooting. This means:

- Tops that cover the front and back of the body (i.e. not strapless)
- Any colour clothing, except for blue denim, olive drab and camouflage patterns

- Plain or specific archery clothing
- Footwear covering the whole foot (no open toed sandals or shoes). You will be on your feet all day and will be doing lots of walking, so make sure they are comfortable and, if possible, waterproof.

And remember, you need your Archery GB membership card. Only Archery GB members can shoot in affiliated tournaments.

At the tournament

Judges are there to help and will be more than happy to answer any questions you have

Arrival: Aim to arrive at least one hour before the start of the event. This will give you time to find out where you are shooting, set up your equipment, and meet your fellow archers.

Registration: When you arrive the first thing to do is to find the booking-in tent. The organiser will check your Archery GB membership card and tell you which target you are shooting on.

Equipment set up: You can then set your equipment up. If you have a tent or a shelter make sure you set it up behind the tent line. There will normally be two lines marked behind the shooting line, the first is the waiting line, the second is the tent line.

Introductions: Introduce yourself to your fellow archers and, if possible, decide whether you want to score or pull the arrows. For your first few shoots you might want to just help pull the arrows and observe the scoring until you feel confident.

Decide where you are going to stand, put foot markers down and to sort out where people want to put their telescopes. Archers are likely to split up into groups or 'details'. If there are four people per detail, archers A and B would be in the first detail and shoot first, followed by C and D.

Assembly: Just before shooting starts there will be an assembly. The time is usually on the entry form. You need to have finished your warm up exercises before the judge or organiser calls everyone together. The organiser will introduce themselves, the judges and any invited guests before going through the practicalities - whether it is five or 10-zone scoring, how many sighters or practice arrows you have and the instructions.

Start: After the assembly finishes, it is time to start shooting. If you have any questions, ask the judge. He or she will be more than happy to answer your questions.

Starting the tournament

Preparation: You will start with either sighters or practice arrows, before scoring begins.

- **Sighters:** These are shot at Archery GB rounds. If you are shooting outdoors it is usually one end of six arrows but if it is an indoor tournament it will probably be two ends of three arrows. This is your only chance to warm up during the tournament. If you decide to shoot two sessions of an indoor Archery GB tournament you will only be able to have sighters at the first session.

- **Practice:** These are shot at World Archery Rounds. You get approximately 20 to 40 minutes of practice which tends to be three ends if shooting in two details outdoors (indoors: usually two ends). You can shoot as many arrows as you want and if you decide to shoot two indoor sessions, you can practise before both.

Most tournaments have their own awards for first, second and third places. There might also be extra prizes such as best gold or worst white!

Scoring: Once everyone has shot their end, there will be three blasts on the whistle to indicate that the archers can go forward to score and collect their arrows.

- Only archers are able to walk to the targets. If someone else wants to walk to the targets they must ask the Judge's permission.

- Make sure you do not touch the target face until all the scores have been written down, otherwise any line cutters will be scored at the lowest value.

- All the archers should gather in front of their target before going to look for missing arrows. The person who is doing the scoring will then call the name of the first archer on the score sheet.

- Scores should be called out in groups of three, starting with the highest score, so for example 9, 9, 7 pause 5, 5, 3. The scorer should repeat the scores back to you.

- When you call out your scores do not touch the arrows. If the shaft of the arrow is touching a dividing line between two scores (a line cutter), it scores the higher score. If you don't agree, then say so, no one will mind. A judge will be called to look at it with a magnifying glass and give a final decision.

- If you make a mistake when calling out your arrows or they are written down incorrectly, call for a judge and ask for the scores to be called again and corrected. Do not do it yourself. You are allowed to alter the adding up.

- The score sheet will probably be passed between a couple of archers because the scorer cannot record their own scores. Or there might be two identical score sheets with two people doing the scoring (double scoring).

- Once all the scores have been recorded, the arrows can be pulled and any missed arrows can be picked up from behind the target.

- Help your target companions pull the arrows and look for any lost arrows. If it is a World Archery round you need to put a small mark against the arrow holes in case of bouncers or 'pass-throughs'.

Equipment failures: If something goes wrong with your equipment, don't panic. Just let a judge know straight away. If you are on the shooting line when it happens, step back and attract the judge's attention. Once everything has been sorted out, the judge will tell you how to catch up with the rest of the archers but you cannot re-shoot any arrows, even if a bad shot was caused by equipment failure.

Bouncers: A bouncer is an arrow that hits the target and rebounds from it. Don't worry if you get one, just stop shooting and call a Judge, who will talk you through what needs to be done.

- **Archery GB round** – Shoot the rest of your arrows, then step off the line and attract the judge's attention. They will ask for a spare arrow, mark it and, when everyone else has finished, get you to shoot it. When you go to score, the judge will come with you just to make sure that the arrow did bounce out. If it did, you get the score of your extra shot. If it hit another arrow, you get the score of that arrow.

- **World Archery round** – Stop shooting and stop everyone else on your target.

Step back and call a judge who will ask you how many arrows you have left to shoot. When everyone else has finished, he or she will stop the shoot and check your target, looking for an unmarked hole. If there is more than one, you get the lowest score. You then go back to the shooting line, finish your end and the judge will check your scores again.

Etiquette

- Be considerate and avoid causing a distraction on the shooting line. Do not walk on or off the line when someone is at full draw and try not to make any comments while on the shooting line, even if you miss.

- Broken arrows can sometimes cause problems. If you hit another arrow in the target, or if you step on a missed arrow that is buried under ground and break it, it is an accident and you are not expected to pay for a replacement. But if you break someone's arrow by being careless, such as not looking where you are going, then the polite thing to do is offer to replace it.
- Do not touch anyone else's bow or equipment without permission.
- Make sure your mobile phone is turned off or is set to silent.
- If the targets need moving, offer to help but don't try to do it alone.
- If you have any problems, or are unsure of what to do then ask a fellow archer or a judge.

Finishing the tournament

At the end of the tournament check your score sheet carefully. Make sure everything is correct and complete all the total boxes, including the number of 'hits' and 'golds'. Once you are happy, sign it. If you think you are eligible for a World Archery or Archery GB award, ask the organiser for a claim form.

Awards

Competition awards: Most tournaments have their own awards for first, second and third places. There might also be extra prizes such as best gold or worst white, judged on one random end of shooting and you won't know which end until you have shot it!

Six Gold End awards: The Six Gold End Badge is an Archery GB award given to people who get six golds at one of the two longest shooting distances. Men can get it for 100 or 80 yards, 90 or 70 metres. Women can get it for 80 or 60 yards, or 70 or 60 metres. There is also a Three Gold End award for longbow archers at the same distance. If you get a six or three gold end ask the organiser for a claim form and send it to the Archery GB Membership Services office.

Archery GB Rose awards: These can only be claimed for York, Hereford, or Bristol tournaments rounds, which have Rose Status and depend on age and gender. Rose Awards recognise scores for recurve and compound archers.

FITA Star awards: Awarded for reaching a certain score at World Record Status tournaments and open to recurve, compound, senior, master or cadet rounds.

A/B/C

Anchor
A consistent reference point of the drawing hand when the bow is at full draw. It is also known as the Reference Point.

Arrow
A projectile shot from a bow.

Arrow rest
A device on which the arrow rests during the draw, located just above the bow handle.

Back (of bow)
The face of the bow that is on the opposite side to the string.

Barebow
A class of shooting that does not permit the use of sights.

Belly (of bow)
The face of the bow which is on the same side as the string.

Boss
A target, to which the target face is pinned. It is usually made of compressed straw or foam.

Bouncer
An arrow that hits the target and rebounds from it.

Bow arm
The arm of the bow hand.

Bow hand
The hand in which the bow is supported.

Bow string
The string which is stretched between the bow nocks when the bow is braced and on which the arrow is placed for shooting.

Bow stringer
A cord with loops or cups on the ends for holding the bow limbs to assist with bracing the bow.

Bracer
A shield or guard worn inside of the forearm of the bow hand, also known as an arm guard.

Bracing height
A specified distance between the string and a particular point on the bow riser.

Button
A button is screwed into the arrow riser and is used to fine tune the arrow flight.

D/E/F

Draw Force Line (DFL)
A straight, imaginary line, from the point of the drawing arm elbow, through the drawing hand to the pressure point where the bow hand contacts the bow at full draw.

Dominant eye
The eye which is preferred by the archer for aiming, when both eyes are open.

Draw
To pull the bow string the full length of the arrow, ready to shoot.

Draw fingers
Normally the first three fingers of the hand, these are used in pulling the string to full draw.

Draw weight
The force measured in pounds, required to pull the bow to a full draw.

Fletch
A feather or vane fitted to an arrow to stabilise it in flight.

Fletchings
A collective word to describe the feathers or vanes on an arrow.

Foot markers
Small discs, of restricted dimensions, used to mark an archer's foot positions.

Follow through
The movements which take place in the archer and their equipment as a result of the release.

Freestyle
Using the recurve bow with the use of a sight, draw length check, pressure button and stabilisers being permitted.

G/H/J

Gold
The central scoring zone of the target, coloured yellow.

Ground quiver
Used in target archery. This is a rod of about 20 inches in length with a loop at the top. The sharp end is stuck into the ground, then arrows are dropped through the loop, standing ready to be used.

Group
A cluster of arrows in a target.

Handle
The part of a bow that is held in the hand.

Hanger
A arrow that does not penetrate into the boss but hangs down from the face.

End
The number of arrows used in scoring a particular target event. In most instances, an end is considered to be six arrows.

Fast
Warning command to stop shooting immediately in the case of a hazard or emergency.

Field captain
Person controlling the shooting along all or part of the shooting range.

Finger tab
A protection worn on the fingers of the string hand, usually made of leather, to protect the fingers and for consistency of release.

Hold

This is a pause by the archer, while at full draw, just before the release of the arrow.

K/L/M

Limbs

The upper and lower working parts of the bow.

N/O/P/Q

Nock

1. The slot in the end of an arrow which is used for clipping it on to the bow string.

2. The grooves at the end of the bow limbs into which is fitted the string.

3. To clip the arrow nock on to the string.

Nocking point

This is the place on the bow string where the nock of the arrow rests.

Over-bowed

This term is used to indicate the instance where the draw weight of the bow is more than the individual archer can draw and shoot with any degree of comfort and efficiency.

Over-braced

The bow being braced to a greater height than that which is efficient.

Overdraw

To draw the pile of the arrow beyond the arrow rest.

Pile

It is the metal tip attached to the head of the arrow shaft: the arrow point.

Pinching

Gripping the nock of the arrow between the fingers when drawing.

Pin-hole

The exact centre of the target; also known as the Spider, and usually marked with a small cross.

Point of aim

This is the point or object at which the archer aims, when they sight over the tip of the arrow. It is also the method of shooting where the arrow is drawn back to the side of the face.

Preparation line

The balanced pre-draw position of the archer. Sometimes related specifically to the relative positions of the bow hand, drawing arm and arrow.

Quiver

The size and shape varies considerably, but this is a holder for arrows so they can be carried ready for quick use. The quiver can be slung over the shoulder on the back, hung from the waist, or a special design attached to the bow.

R/S/T

Recurve

A recurve bow has tips that curve away from the archer when the bow is strung.

Reference point

The place where the arrow drawing hand positions itself on the face. It is also known as the Anchor Point.

Riser

The rigid centre section of a bow on to which the working limbs are joined.

Rounds
The designated number of arrows shot at a given distance or standardised series of distances.

Shooting line
The line the archer stands astride when shooting.

Sling
Used to restrain the bow from jumping out of the hand when shooting with a relaxed bow hand.

Spectator line
A designated area behind the shooting line where spectators watch.

String
Bow string.

T-Draw
Basic technique used by coaches to teach beginners Barebow and Freestyle shooting.

Take down bow
The type of bow that the limbs can be removed for transportation or even to change the draw weight of the bow by changing the limbs.

Target face
A cover marked with the scoring zones, placed over the target boss. Usually made of a reinforced paper.

Target stand
A stand supporting the boss.

Trajectory
The curved flight of the arrow caused by the effect of gravity while the arrow is in flight.

U/V/W/Y/Z

Under-bowed
The situation where an archer has a bow that is too light in draw weight.

Under-draw
Not to draw sufficient arrow length.

Unit aiming
Maintaining the relationship of the arms, head and shoulders by adjusting the aiming from the waist.

Waiting line
A line located behind the shooting line, where archers wait while others are shooting.

World Archery
The international governing body for archery also known as Federation Internationale de Tir à l'Arc or 'FITA'.

Thank you to the following people who have contributed to the development and publication of this guidebook.

Co-authors:
Hannah Bussey
Jane Percival

Technical author:
Andy Hood

Executive sponsor:
Bob McGonigle

Acknowledgements:
Katy Lipscomb
Joe Ground
Jennifer Kimber
Graham Harris
Ollie Holt

Photography:
Keiron Tovell
Dean Alberga
Rob Finney
John Percival
Paul Pickard

Archery GB
Lilleshall National Sports &
Conferencing Centre
Newport
Shropshire TF10 9AT

**You can reach us on the web/
facebook/twitter at:**
www.archerygb.org
www.facebook.com/archerygb
www.twitter.com/archerygb

Telephone:
01952 677888

Email:
enquiries@archerygb.org

THE ARCHERY FOR BEGINNERS GUIDEBOOK

IMPORTANT PLEASE READ THIS !!

Thank you for purchasing your bow from Archery Supplies Direct, but before you use it please make sure you carefully read the following as failure to do so could result in injury and expensive repair bills.

Please note – Strings do NOT snap/derail under normal use and are NOT covered by any manufacturers warranty. When used correctly the arrow ensures that there is sufficient drag to reduce the kinetic energy of the string down to a speed that will not cause it to break. The reasons for snapped / derailment of strings are:

· Firing the bow with no arrow in place – NEVER do this *
· Not using the correct arrows.
· Over drawing the string can cause the cams to break.

Failure to follow these rules could result in a dry fire and serious damage to your bow (broken string and damaged limbs). This is not covered in your warranty and is easily spotted by our engineers so please do not return your "dry fired" bow and claim it to be faulty. Strings do not snap on correct firing, strings fray and unravel but give you plenty of warning to replace, they are not covered by our manufacturers warranty.

If you have any questions please contact us on 01527 759339

Our Bows and arrows are security marked and traceable, we will cooperate with the police in providing customer details in cases when required to do so.

www.archerysuppliesdirect.co.uk

ASD Distribution Ltd
T/A
Archery Supplies Direct

60 Arthur St,
Unit 6, Victor Business Centre,
Lakeside
Redditch
B98 8JY

Tel: 01527 759339